A Kid's Mensch Handbook
Step by Step to a Lifetime of Jewish Values

by Scott E. Blumenthal

Behrman House Publishers
www.behrmanhouse.com

Book and Cover Design: **Russell Cohen**
"Izzy" Illustrations: **Jim Steck**

The publisher and author gratefully acknowledge the following sources of photographs and graphic images:

Creative Image 41, 67, 81; **Dan Farrall\Photodisc\PictureQuest** 8; **Gila Gevirtz** 17;
Brownie Harris/CORBIS 12; **Katherine Schwartz** 33; **Israeli Scouts** 108; **Jewish Museum of Maryland**
109; **Richard Lobell** 30; **LWA-Dann Tardiff/CORBIS** 105; **Sheila Plotkin** 28; **Beverly Weiss** 74;
Sunny Yellen 53, 91

Published by Behrman House, Inc.
Springfield, NJ 07081
www.behrmanhouse.com

Library of Congress Cataloging-in-Publication Data

Blumenthal, Scott.
  A kid's mensch handbook : step by step to a lifetime of Jewish values / Scott E. Blumenthal.
      p. cm.
  Includes index.
  ISBN 0-87441-700-7
  1. Jewish ethics–Juvenile literature. 2. Conduct of life–Juvenile literature. 3. Commandments
(Judaism)–Juvenile literature. 4. Jewish way of life–Juvenile literature. I. Title.

  BJ1285.B56 2004
  296.7'083–dc22

                                        2004046344

Manufactured in Canada

To my brother Matthew,
a real mensch

Table of Contents

Part One: The Mensch Basics

Part Two: Be a Mensch to Yourself

Part Three: Be a Mensch to Others

Izzy, the Mensch-in-Training

SEE YOU INSIDE!

Part One
The Mensch Basics

Chapter 1

Welcome to *A Kid's Mensch Handbook*

What *is* a mensch, anyway?

How can I be someone people respect?

What's *A Kid's Mensch Handbook* all about?

Chapter 2

Making Mensch Choices

Why is making good choices an important Jewish value?

What are some examples of good choices?

How can *I* make good choices?

Chapter 3

Taking Mensch Actions

I've made some good choices. Now what?

What's a mitzvah? How is it different from a good deed?

Why is "love your neighbor as yourself" the most important mitzvah?

Chapter 1

Welcome to A Kid's Mensch Handbook

Actions

Choices

Integrity

Respect

The Ripple Effect

Making Waves

If you drop a stone into a still lake, there will be a *plunk!*, then a *splash!*, then—rolling outward in perfect circles—ripples. Imagine that you are the stone. Those around you—family, friends, classmates, even strangers you'll never meet—are the lake. And your actions, which radiate far beyond you, to places you can hardly see, are the ripples.

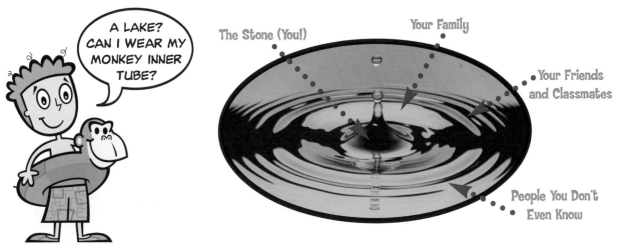

A LAKE? CAN I WEAR MY MONKEY INNER TUBE?

The Stone (You!)

Your Family

Your Friends and Classmates

People You Don't Even Know

Each of us, Judaism teaches, affects the world in profound and extraordinary ways. Our actions affect those around us—and make a difference in people's lives. Maimonides, the great rabbi and philosopher, challenged us to imagine that even a single action could "tip the balance, our own balance and the balance of the entire world." In short, our actions *matter*.

QUICK QUOTE **People are honored for their wisdom but loved for their kindness.**
—*Shalom Hacohen, Polish writer*

Of course, some actions affect the world in not-so-profound ways. You can affect those around you by slurping hot chocolate in the library. Or make a difference in people's lives by e-mailing a virus to everyone on your address list. But that isn't exactly what Maimonides had in mind. Instead, our challenge is to take action that is generous and kind, action that affects others in positive ways, action that makes you—in your own eyes and in the eyes of your community—a mensch.

I'VE ALWAYS WANTED TO BE A MENSCH—WHATEVER THAT IS.

That's Fine and Dandy, but What *Is* a Mensch?

Why is it that "you are such a mensch" is one of the greatest compliments a person can receive? *Mensch* is a Yiddish word that simply means "person." And everyone is a person, no matter how good or bad, honest or rotten. However, the word *mensch* has come to mean much, much more. So much more, in fact, that it's almost impossible to define it in just a few words. So we'll use many:

✦ **A mensch is a person who is honest and fair—a person of *integrity*.**

✦ **A mensch is a person who shares the last slice of pizza, recycles the soda cans, and helps to clean up—without being asked—when the party is over.**

✦ **A mensch is a person who shows respect for himself or herself and for others, and so is respected *by* others.**

✦ **A mensch is, quite simply, a good person.**

✦ **A mensch understands that he or she, like a stone in a lake, has the power to affect the world in amazing ways.**

The star of **A Kid's Mensch Handbook** *is you.*

In a nutshell, that's what *A Kid's Mensch Handbook* is all about.

Too Many to Menschen

Think of three people you consider *menschen* (*menschen* means "more than one mensch"): someone at school, someone at home, and someone who is famous. Write their names on the lines below. Then, explain why each one is a mensch.

Names:

someone at school	someone at home	someone who is famous

Reasons each one is a mensch:

A Kid's Mensch Handbook in a Nutshell

A Kid's Mensch Handbook was created with *you* in mind. It's chock-full of helpful hints, good advice, and timeless Jewish wisdom to help you become a top-notch, gold-medal mensch. On the way, you'll find fun questions, quick quizzes, and sample situations to guide you along your *own* path to mensch-hood. (Because, as you'll see, no two paths are the same.)

I HAVE A MAP TO MENSCH-HOOD. OR IS IT A MAP TO MONTANA?

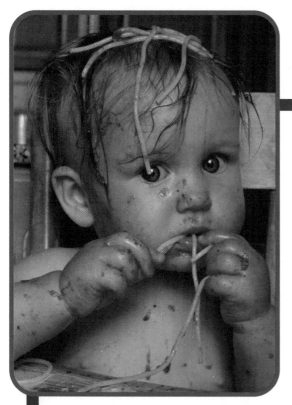

BABY MENSCH

Circle the answer that best completes the following passage.

A legend from the Talmud explains that when a baby is born, an angel appears. The angel requires that the baby take an important oath, that the goal of his or her life will be to

    a. wear cute clothing

    b. excel at trivia games

    c. eat as much spaghetti as possible

    d. be a good person

ANSWER: If you answered anything but d, put gum on your nose and stand in the corner.

A Kid's Mensch Handbook is divided into three parts:

I. The Mensch Basics

In order to be a mensch, you've got to make *good choices*, then take *action*. We'll spend one chapter talking about each. (What do *you* do when a friend is sick? We'll talk about why it matters.)

II. Be a Mensch to Yourself

The great rabbi Hillel said, "If I am not for myself, who will be for me?" In Part Two, we'll talk about an extremely important person: you. You'll learn that all people are created *b'tzelem Elohim* (in God's image) and what that has to do with washing behind your ears. You'll learn how to look in the mirror and say, "Hey, that's one serious mensch."

III. Be a Mensch to Others

Hillel added, "If I am only for myself, what am I?" In Part Three, we'll shift our focus from how you affect *you* to how you affect *others*. You'll discover ways to be a mensch to just about everybody, including your family, your friends, even the population of Guatemala.

While We're at It

As you explore *A Kid's Mensch Handbook*, you'll find answers to other questions you may have about your heritage, including these:

✔ What does it mean to be Jewish?

✔ What makes me Jewish?

✔ Why should I be proud of being Jewish?

Chapter 2

Making Mensch Choices

Hard Decisions

Questions

Answers

Wisdom

Choices, Choices!

The New-Kid Dilemma, Part 1

Imagine this. You're in school, about to eat lunch. You're sitting with kids you know—some who are friends, some who are *sort of* friends. Everyone is laughing and talking about a show that was on TV the night before. Just as you're about to chomp into your peanut butter and jelly sandwich, you notice the new kid, Alex, sitting alone at the next table. "That's all we need," says your friend next to you, "another new kid." "Yeah," says another, "we've got way too many kids in our class already."

As you watch Alex eat, quickly and quietly, you remember how you felt when you were the new kid—nervous, confused, and lonely. You would have done anything to sit and have fun with the other kids. You consider inviting Alex to join you. But what would the others think? Would you make a fool of yourself? And anyway, what would you say?

What would *you* choose to do?

IF I MAKE FRIENDS WITH ALEX, DO I HAVE TO SHARE MY SANDWICH?

 **QUICK QUOTE** **No one is alone in the spirit of Judaism.**
—*Henrietta Szold, founder of Hadassah*

The New-Kid Choice Chart

1. Choose a starting point—A or B. Follow the arrows to each of Alex's responses and each long-term result.
2. Now, go in the opposite direction. Choose the long-term result you like best, and work backward. Which starting action—A or B—must you take in order to reach the outcome you want? _____

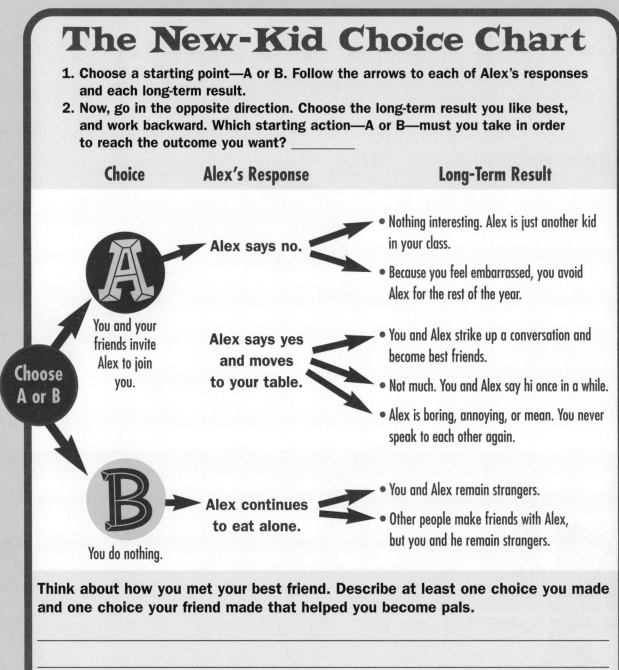

Choice	Alex's Response	Long-Term Result

Choose A or B

A
You and your friends invite Alex to join you.

Alex says no.
- Nothing interesting. Alex is just another kid in your class.
- Because you feel embarrassed, you avoid Alex for the rest of the year.

Alex says yes and moves to your table.
- You and Alex strike up a conversation and become best friends.
- Not much. You and Alex say hi once in a while.
- Alex is boring, annoying, or mean. You never speak to each other again.

B
You do nothing.

Alex continues to eat alone.
- You and Alex remain strangers.
- Other people make friends with Alex, but you and he remain strangers.

Think about how you met your best friend. Describe at least one choice you made and one choice your friend made that helped you become pals.

_____
_____
_____
_____

The Choice Is Yours

Our choices are important. They affect who we are, how others see us, even how we see ourselves. Our choices affect those around us, including our families, our friends, our communities, and the whole world. They can affect our health and our happiness. They can even change the future. Choices lead to action.

Choosing an ice cream flavor may not be such a big choice. But some choices, especially those that involve other people, are more difficult.

When it comes to making tough choices, you are not alone. For generations, our ancestors have wrestled with tough choices and have asked the same questions that you do: Does dropping coins into the tzedakah box make a difference? Should I stay angry with my friend forever, or is it okay to forgive and forget? If Phyllis got a bad haircut, should I tell her it looks nice anyway? Sometimes our ancestors made good choices; sometimes they made bad ones. They were not so different from us.

Sometimes our ancestors made choices that were worth remembering, writing down, and passing on to their children. For generations, rabbis, parents, teachers, philosophers, sometimes even kids like you, have passed on thoughts and suggestions that can help us—and future generations—make good choices.

QUICK QUOTE **Days are scrolls; write on them what you choose.**
—*Rabbi Baḥya ibn Pakuda, Spanish writer*

Three Cheers, Three Jeers

List three good choices you've made this year:

1. _____

_____

_____

_____

2. _____

_____

_____

_____

3. _____

_____

_____

_____

List three not-so-good choices:

1. _____

_____

_____

_____

2. _____

_____

_____

_____

3. _____

_____

_____

_____

Good Choice!

We know that the choices we make are important. We know that they are often difficult. We also know that a choice may be right for one person but not for another. So now the question is: How do we make good choices? The answer: in lots of ways.

Some good choices we just *stumble* on. They are based on observation, everyday experience, even mistakes we've made before. After the first Stone Age cave man stuck his hand in fire, for example, the choice was clear: *Do not stick your hand in fire.* Or as the Talmud tells us, "One must not go into a building that is in ruins." The ancient rabbis collected this wisdom, these good choices, and passed it from one generation to the next. The goal was to help their children, their children's children, and us, live happier, safer, more meaningful lives.

I'VE MADE A GOOD CHOICE. NO BROCCOLI.

Some choices we arrive at after a great deal of thought and reflection. For example, there's the famous "eye for an eye" rule. According to the Torah, the punishment for a person who hurts someone should be "an eye for an eye, a tooth for a tooth." Does that mean that if someone pokes your eye out, you should poke out theirs? The rabbis of the Talmud argued that no, the Torah doesn't mean that at all. Instead, they decided, the guilty person should pay a fine based on the seriousness of the injury. If we took "an eye for an eye" literally, then two people would end up blind—and that would solve nothing.

Some choices are still up in the air—we don't really know what the best answers are. Those choices vary from community to community and from person to person. Some hot debate topics include:

✦ **What is the best way to achieve peace in Israel?**

✦ **Should cloning of human organs be allowed?**

✦ **Should prayers be recited in Hebrew only, or are other languages acceptable?**

Each of us—even you!—can participate in the ongoing quest for good choices.

Mensch-Wise

Here's an example of a choice that may sound familiar:

Suppose you see someone accidentally drop her books, papers, pens, pencils, and a bag of marbles in the hallway. Suppose it's someone you don't like, maybe someone who doesn't like you. What would *you* do? Why?

_____

_____

_____

_____

Answers, Answers!

Torah, Talmud, and Beyond

In time, our ancestors had collected so many good choices of every kind that they needed to organize and preserve them so that future generations—so that *you*—could learn from their examples. (That's one of the best things about being Jewish: We've got thousands of years of experience and wisdom to help guide us through our lives.) These are the most important sources of good Jewish choices:

Tanach. The roots of our tradition are found in the Hebrew Bible, the Tanach. The Tanach includes the five books of the Torah, the books of the Prophets (such as Isaiah and Jonah), and the books of Writings (including the story of Esther, which we read on Purim). The Tanach contains laws to help us make tough choices, as well as stories about how our ancestors, such as Abraham, Rebecca, King Solomon, and Ruth, made *their* tough choices.

Talmud. Later, great rabbis studied the Tanach to learn how best to live their lives. Their good choices and their arguments *about* those choices (like us, they didn't always agree) were recorded in a set of volumes called the Talmud. *Talmud* means "learning." The Talmud records what these great rabbis learned from one another, and what we can learn from them.

Midrashim. For centuries, people have written stories to better understand why people like Moses and Rebecca and Joseph made the choices they did. These stories and the lessons they teach us are called *midrashim*. Because people continue to create *midrashim* every day, gathering all of them in a single volume would be a never-ending task. In fact, some *midrashim* aren't in books at all; they're in magazines, in sermons, even on the Internet.

The New-Kid Dilemma, Part 2

Another source of good choices is one that was created just for you: this book.
Here's an example. Remember Alex, the new kid from the beginning of the
chapter? When it comes to how we should treat guests and strangers—including
new kids in our school—Judaism's choice is clear:

In the Torah, we read of three guests who arrived at Abraham and Sarah's doorstep.
Immediately Abraham and Sarah sprang into action. They brought water so that their
guests could wash their feet (they *were* in the desert, you know) and invited them to
recline under a shady tree. They selected a sheep from their flock and prepared a
great feast. They opened their home and their hearts to the strangers, who were soon
no longer strangers.

So the next time Alex—or someone like Alex—turns up in your class, you'll know
what Judaism says you should do. And it doesn't have to involve washing feet.
A simple "Hello, my name is . . ." will do.

You're Welcome!

One of Judaism's most important commandments, *hachnasat orḥim*—bringing
in guests—teaches the importance of welcoming strangers and visitors. Write
about a time in your life when *you* welcomed someone. How did you feel? How
did the person react?

_____

_____

_____

_____

WISDOM FROM THE OLD COUNTRY

Yiddish proverbs provide more good choices—and timeless Jewish advice. Here are a few Yiddish proverbs that you might have heard in the marketplace of a *shtetl* (a village in eastern Europe) two hundred years ago:

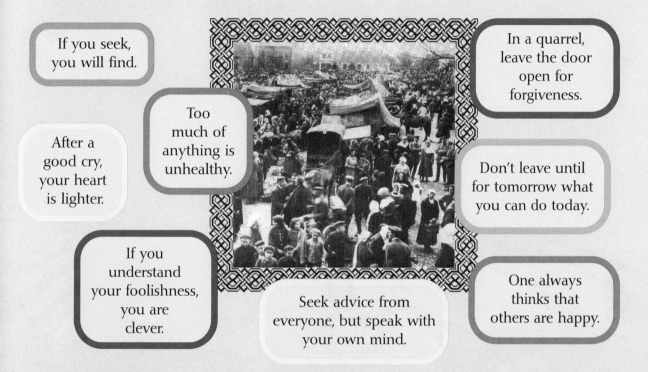

If you seek, you will find.

After a good cry, your heart is lighter.

Too much of anything is unhealthy.

If you understand your foolishness, you are clever.

Seek advice from everyone, but speak with your own mind.

In a quarrel, leave the door open for forgiveness.

Don't leave until for tomorrow what you can do today.

One always thinks that others are happy.

Some Yiddish proverbs are like riddles—they don't mean exactly what they say. For example, "If you don't eat garlic, you won't smell bad." In other words, don't do something that you know is harmful.

Another Yiddish proverb warns us, "Don't rub salt into a wound." What do you think *that* proverb means?

_____

_____

_____

Chapter 3
Taking Mensch Actions

Mitzvot

The Golden Rule

Middot

Generosity

The Action Reaction

Starting Small

Rachel had made up her mind: She would help end world hunger. Not next week, not in seventh grade. *Now*. "There are too many hungry people," she announced to her family. "And I've chosen to help."

"You're only eleven," said her annoying big brother. "What can *you* do about it?"

"A lot," said Rachel as she stormed off to the TV room, where she flopped down on the couch and finished off a bag of potato chips.

"What happened to world hunger?" asked Rachel's grandmother, an hour later.

"What about it?" asked Rachel, holding her aching belly.

"Weren't you going to help end it?"

"Probably."

"Well, what are you going to *do*?"

"I'm going to help. Isn't that enough?"

BURP.

Rachel's grandmother smiled. "I'll be right back," she said. Minutes later she returned with an empty oatmeal container, colored paper, and a bunch of markers.

"What's that?" asked Rachel.

"Tools to help end world hunger," replied her grandmother.

As they sat together, turning the oatmeal container into a purple and yellow (Rachel's favorite colors) tzedakah box, Rachel and her grandmother wrote a list of ideas:

✔ The money we collect will go to Mazon, a Jewish organization that distributes food to hungry people.

✔ Next week, we will help make sandwiches for hungry and homeless people at the synagogue's Mitzvah Day.

✔ When spring comes, we will donate packets of vegetable seeds to the local homeless shelter so that the people there can plant a garden and help feed themselves.

"Thanks, Grandma, but I've got to run," Rachel said, placing the tzedakah box on the kitchen counter. "I've decided to create world peace. And I've got *a lot* to do."

QUICK QUOTE **Wisdom without action is like a tree without fruit.**
—*Joseph Kimḥi, Spanish poet*

THE MITZVAH MARVEL

Secret identity: You are the cunning and courageous Mitzvah Marvel.

Special power: You never miss a mitzvah, an opportunity to help others.

Your mission: It's a busy Sunday. Everywhere you go, there's a mitzvah to be performed. Respond to each "Choice Challenge" by describing the "Action" you would take.

TIME OF DAY	CHOICE CHALLENGE	MITZVAH OPPORTUNITY	ACTION
9:51 a.m.	Two religious school classmates are having an argument. Voices are being raised. Names are being called. It's getting worse and worse.	*rodef shalom* (make peace when you can)	
11:35 a.m.	Your religious school is having a car wash to raise money for the homeless. Your classmates need one more volunteer to grab a soapy sponge.	*tzedakah* (give to those in need)	
2:33 p.m.	Two people on your soccer team refer to a teammate as "stupid" after she misses a goal. They are waiting for you to join in agree.	*l'shon hara* (avoid gossip)	
4:07 p.m.	Your friend has chicken pox. You've had it already, so you know it's not fun. You talk to him on the phone, and he sounds miserable.	*bikkur ḥolim* (visit the sick)	

27

Mitzvah Your Way to Mensch-hood

We know that it's important to make good choices. But the choice to feed the hungry doesn't fill someone's stomach. The choice to be a team player doesn't help to score the winning goal. The choice to be a good friend doesn't help a classmate through a sad time. Once we've made a choice, Judaism tells us, we must take *action*.

Judaism has a word for an action that follows good choices: mitzvah.

A mensch chooses to do the stinky laundry that's been under the bed for a month—and actually does it.

A mitzvah is more than just a good deed. It is, the Torah tells us, a commandment from God. So when we perform a mitzvah, we involve not only ourselves (the mitzvah do-ers) and others (the mitzvah receivers) but also God (the mitzvah maker). That's how important *mitzvot* (more than one mitzvah) are.

Mitzvah Twins

In fact, there are two types of *mitzvot*: ritual and ethical. Ritual *mitzvot* have to do with, among other things, prayer (recite a blessing before eating), *kashrut* (stay away from cheeseburgers), and the Bible (read the story of Jonah—and the big fish that swallowed him—on Yom Kippur). Ethical *mitzvot* have to do with treating people, including ourselves, with *kavod*—respect. In *A Kid's Mensch Handbook*, we'll talk about *ethical* mitzvot.

QUICK QUOTE One mitzvah leads to another.
—*Pirkei Avot 4:2*

A Vote for Mitzvot

The Torah contains hundreds of *mitzvot*, some of which you already do every day: Learning in school is a mitzvah. Speaking respectfully to your parents is a mitzvah. Even taking care of yourself by brushing your teeth is a mitzvah. Almost any time you help yourself or someone else improve, it's a mitzvah.

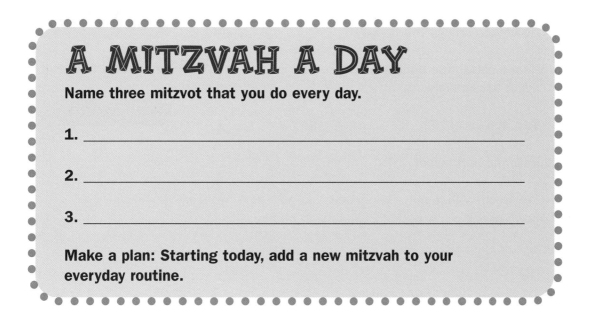

A MITZVAH A DAY

Name three mitzvot that you do every day.

1. _____

2. _____

3. _____

Make a plan: Starting today, add a new mitzvah to your everyday routine.

Other *mitzvot* you perform once in a while or when opportunities arise. For example, you visit a friend who is ill, donate clothing to a homeless shelter, or welcome a guest into your home. For those *mitzvot*, you need to keep your mensch radar up—you never know when the chance to perform a mitzvah will come along.

Mitzvah Calendar

Connect each mitzvah on the left to the frequency with which you perform it on the right.

Visit a sick friend.

Do chores around the house.

Help a classmate understand his or her schoolwork.

Say "I'm sorry."

Return a lost object.

Almost every day

About once a week

A few times a year

Which mitzvah is more important: one you perform every day or one you perform once in a while? Explain your choice.

_____

_____

_____

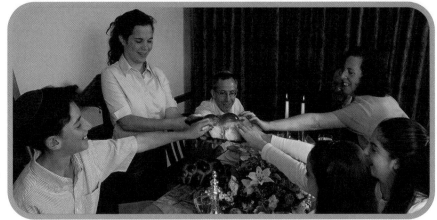

Sharing is a mitzvah we can perform every day.

MENSCH
SPOTLIGHT

Name: Naḥshon ben Aminadav, of the tribe of Judah

Scene: It is thousands of years ago, just as the Israelites have been freed from slavery in Egypt. They arrive at the Sea of Reeds. Behind them is the Egyptian army, rushing to capture their former slaves and return them to slavery.

The Israelites complain to Moses: "Why did we leave Egypt, only to come out here and die?"

God instructs Moses to stretch his hand over the sea. Moses obeys, but nothing happens. Moses orders the Israelites to move forward, but they do not; they are too afraid. God waits for a sign of faith.

Action: According to a *midrash*, Naḥshon ben Aminadav knows that the only way to rescue his people is through action. He steps forward and places a toe into the sea. Nothing happens. He continues walking until the water is up to his waist. Nothing. To his shoulders. Nothing. To his chin. Still nothing. Finally, just as the water reaches Naḥshon's lips, the sea bursts open and the children of Israel walk to safety.

What made Naḥshon a mensch: The midrash tells us that Naḥshon's action proved to God that the Israelites had faith.

It's a fact: For generations, Naḥshon has been a symbol of courage for Jews. There is even a Hebrew word from Naḥshon's name, *naḥshoni*, meaning "daring" or "brave."

The All-in-One Mitzvah

On One Foot

The Torah contains five books. Near the middle of the third book, Vayikra, we find what may be the most important mitzvah of them all: *v'ahavta l'reacha kamocha*, or "love your neighbor as yourself." The Golden Rule.

The Talmud tells this story: A Roman soldier approached the great rabbi Hillel. "I will convert to Judaism if you can teach me the entire Torah while I stand on one foot," he said. Hillel replied, "What is hateful to yourself, do not do to your neighbor. That is the whole Torah; the rest is commentary. Now go and learn."

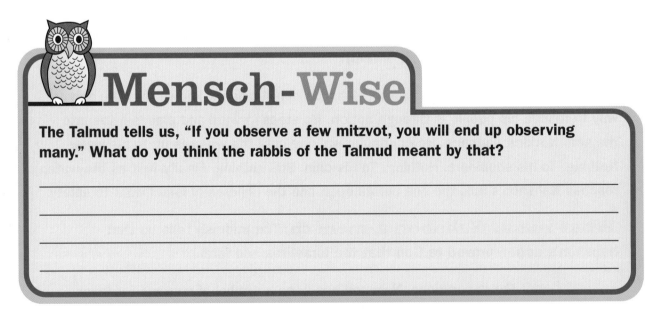

Mensch-Wise

The Talmud tells us, "If you observe a few mitzvot, you will end up observing many." What do you think the rabbis of the Talmud meant by that?

_____

_____

_____

_____

Why did Hillel choose *that* mitzvah and not the commandment to give tzedakah, to respect our elders, or to visit the sick? The answer is this: He didn't need to. His mitzvah includes them all.

Hillel's mitzvah is *v'ahavta l'reacha kamocha*.

Let's look at *v'ahavta l'reacha kamocha* under the Mensch-ifying Glass:

✳ You may recognize *v'ahavta* from the prayer service. We say, *V'ahavta et Adonai elohecha*—You shall love Adonai your God—after we recite the Sh'ma.

✳ *L'reacha* comes from the word *re'a*, meaning "another person." We usually translate *l'reacha* as "your neighbor."

✳ *Kamocha* means "like you" or "as yourself."

So . . . *v'ahavta l'reacha kamocha* means "love your neighbor as yourself."

וְאָהַבְתָּ לְרֵעֲךָ כָּמוֹךָ

CAN I GET DOWN NOW?

The Golden Rule can help us to be good friends.

Falling into Place

"It is a mitzvah to visit the sick, to console the mourner, and to escort one's guest," said Maimonides, the great Jewish philosopher. "Though all of these *mitzvot* are a matter of law, they are nevertheless included in the verse 'You shall love your neighbor as yourself.'" When we perform the mitzvah of *v'ahavta l'reacha kamocha*, all other *mitzvot* seem to fall into place.

One More Time!

Think of a time in your life when someone did *not* treat you according to the principles of *v'ahavta l'reacha kamocha*. How did you feel? Do you wish you had acted differently? If so, how?

_____

_____

_____

Think of a time when someone *did* treat you according to the principles of *v'ahavta l'reacha kamocha*. How did you feel then? What do you wish that person had done differently? Explain your response.

_____

_____

_____

A Note of Middot

Mitzvot tell us what we need to do to become *menschen*. *Middot* (virtues or values) tell us <u>how</u> we can become *menschen*. For example, we know that tzedakah is a mitzvah, a commandment. But in what way should we give tzedakah? With the *middot* of *n'divut* (generosity), *ḥesed* (kindness), and *simḥah* (joy).

GENEROSITY

Based on the middah: "a good heart"

Think about it: In ancient times, the *leiv*—heart—was thought to be the source of compassion and generosity. Why? Because just as the heart is necessary to sustain the body, so is generosity necessary to sustain the community. If you could have asked Maimonides, he might have told you that the purpose of all *mitzvot* is the creation of *leiv tov*—a good and generous heart.

Remember it: We see examples of generosity everywhere in Judaism, from the donations the Israelites made to build the Tabernacle in the wilderness, to *mishlo'ah-manot* (baskets of *hamantashen* and other treats) on Purim, to giving gifts during Hanukkah. Generosity is a great way to practice *v'ahavta l'reacha kamocha*, loving our neighbors as ourselves. But you don't need an excuse to be generous. A mensch is generous for the sake of being generous.

Part Two
Be a Mensch to Yourself

Chapter 4

Seeing Yourself as a Mensch

What does self-respect have to do with being a mensch?

Why should I respect myself?

What does it mean to be created *b'tzelem Elohim*—in God's image?

Chapter 5

Treating Yourself as a Mensch

Why is the body "the soul's house"?

How does *sh'mirat habriyut*—guarding one's health—help me to respect myself?

How can I take care of my body *and* my mind?

Chapter 4

Seeing Yourself as a Mensch

Self-respect

Contentment

Compassion

Balance

Pleased to Meet Me

The Mensch-Cam

You have been chosen to test a new and extraordinary invention: the mensch-cam. The mensch-cam is an invisible camera that captures your daily activities: brushing your teeth, feeding your hamster, whispering a secret *that no one should know*. Now, imagine that it follows you for one week and creates a two-hour mensch movie, which contains the memorable—and not-so-memorable—highlights of your week. (Fortunately, the mensch movie contains a digital eye scan; no one can watch it but you.)

The following Sunday, your mensch movie is ready. You pop it in, flop back on the couch, and munch anxiously on a bag of popcorn. Some parts make you laugh. Others make you cringe. Others surprise you: Am I *that* mean to my brother? Wow—my trombone playing is really coming along. Whew—I'm glad I cleaned *that* up.

Two hours later, you see yourself in a whole new way. It's as if you'd met yourself for the first time. You realize that you're the hero—and the author—of your life story. You realize that you have the power to help, hurt, and influence those around you. You realize that you are an important person.

PERSONALLY, I CAN'T GET OVER HOW CUTE I AM.

QUICK QUOTE First become a blessing to yourself so that you may be a blessing to others. —*Rabbi Samson Raphael Hirsch, German scholar*

MENSCH MOVIE REVIEW

Imagine that you've just watched *your* mensch movie, which recorded the highlights of the past week. Do you wish you had done anything differently? Do you want to see it again, or never again? Complete the "Mensch Movie Review" to discover some answers.

Which three scenes from your mensch movie are you most proud of?

1. _____

2. _____

3. _____

Which three scenes do you wish you could do over?

1. _____

2. _____

3. _____

Would you say that the hero of your mensch movie (you!) treated him or herself with respect? Explain your answer.

_____

_____

_____

_____

An Eye That Sees

Actually, our sages imagined a mensch-cam long before cameras existed—about two thousand years before. In *Pirkei Avot*, a collection of wisdom and sayings of ancient Jewish scholars, we read, "Know what is above you: an eye that sees and an ear that hears." *Pirkei Avot* reminds us that God pays attention. It also reminds us to examine ourselves and to challenge ourselves to make choices and take actions that will make us proud.

That's why Part Two of *A Kid's Mensch Handbook*—the part about being a mensch to yourself—begins with a chapter on *self-respect*.

Being a mensch helps us to like what we see in the mirror.

I Know What You Mean

Imagine that your friend's grandmother just died. You pay a *shiva* call (a visit to a house of mourning) and see your friend crying. You didn't know your friend's grandmother, so you don't feel sad in the same way. But you *do* know what it's like to feel sad. That's because our experiences help us to understand our friend's feelings and emotions.

The same is true of self-respect. When we understand how it feels to respect *ourselves*, we better understand how others feel when we respect *them*.

The Divine Spark

In God's Image

Human beings are unique among God's creations. Though trees, birds, fish, and even creepy-crawly insects are valuable and deserve our respect, only we were created *b'tzelem Elohim*—in God's image.

Let's take a look at those two super-important words under the Mensch-ifying Glass:

* ✳ The word *b'tzelem* means "in the likeness of" or "in the image of."
* ✳ *Elohim* means "God." We hear this word in a different form when we say, *Eloheinu Melech ha'olam*, "Our God, Ruler of the universe."
* ✳ We usually translate *b'tzelem Elohim* as "in the image of God" or "in God's image."

בְּצֶלֶם
אֱלֹהִים

But what does it mean to be created "in God's image"? The words suggest that in some way, we are like God. But how? Do we look like God? Can we, like God, create oceans and mountains? Are we, as in the words of the rabbis, the "shield of salvation in every generation"? Probably not. But perhaps there are other ways in which we *are* like God.

> I CAN MAKE A PRETTY BIG SAND CASTLE. DOES THAT COUNT?

The Breath of Life

One way in which we are like God may be found in the Torah: "God formed the human of the dust of the ground and breathed into the human's nostrils the breath of life, and the human became a living soul." We each possess a soul, a *nefesh*, that sets us apart from God's other creations. It reminds us that we can be—in many ways—like God. But how?

◆ Like God, we can be holy. Unlike other living things, we can perform *mitzvot*: We can read, write, and study; we can recite blessings to make our everyday lives more sacred and meaningful.

◆ Like God, we can create. We can create books from blank sheets of paper; we can create art from lumps of clay; we can create skyscrapers from steel, brick, and glass.

◆ Like God, we can tell the difference between right and wrong. We can be truthful with our family and friends; we can stand up for someone who is being picked on; we can share the last cookie rather than gobbling it up ourselves.

 **QUICK QUOTE** **The soul is a tiny lamp kindled by God's light.**
—*Talmud, Shabbat 33a*

Mensch-Wise

In your own words, explain what it means to be created *b'tzelem Elohim*— in God's image.

_____

_____

_____

Two Pockets

Rabbi Simḥah Bunim made this suggestion to his congregation:

Let each of us carry two pieces of paper in our pockets.

The first piece of paper should contain this quotation from the Talmud: "For me the world was created." That is, each of us is unique and vital to the universe, with a value beyond measure.

The second piece of paper should contain these words from the Torah: "I am but dust and ashes." Though we were created by God, we are not God. We are mortal, we have much to learn, and we are far from perfect.

When we achieve a balance between these two ideas, we discover the true meaning of self-respect.

Our sages have called the soul a "divine spark" that exists within each of us. Of course we should respect ourselves—each of us contains a spark of God.

B'TZELEM ELOHIM TOP 5

Here are five ways to build your self-respect muscles:

1 TAKE STOCK

A great way to build self-respect is by asking yourself *about* yourself. Take this short *b'tzelem Elohim* quiz. Place a ✔ next to each statement that describes you. (You may ✔ one or both statements in each pair.) Place a ☺ next to statements you'd like to work on.

___ I'm careful about treating myself with respect.

___ I do only what I believe is right.

___ I often go along with the crowd, even if I think they're doing something wrong.

___ I often do things I'm proud of.

___ I usually try hard to consider other people's feelings.

___ I often do things that make me say "Oops!"

___ I usually care only about my own feelings.

___ I often forget to take care of myself.

2 BE KIND

Another way you can be like God is by showing compassion, kindness, and understanding.

Write some ways in which you can show compassion, kindness, or understanding during the coming week . . .

AT HOME: _____
_____
_____
_____

IN SCHOOL: _____
_____
_____
_____

BY YOURSELF: _____
_____
_____
_____

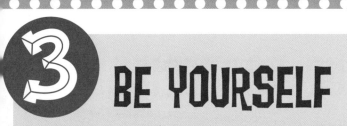

BE YOURSELF

A famous Jewish legend tells the story of Reb Zusya:

> The students of Reb Zusya came to their teacher, who lay dying. They were surprised to see him trembling with fear.
>
> "Why are you afraid of death?" they asked. "In your life, have you not been as righteous as Moses himself?"
>
> "When I stand before the throne of judgment," Zusya answered, "I will not be asked, 'Reb Zusya, why were you not like Moses?' I will be asked, 'Reb Zusya, why were you not like Zusya?'"

It's hard to respect yourself if you're trying to be someone else.

Tell about a time when you chose to do what you felt was right rather than follow the crowd. How did you feel?

_____

_____

_____

_____

_____

4 RECHARGE YOUR BATTERIES

One of the best ways to reflect on your actions (and decide how to handle tough situations) is by taking some time every day to be by yourself. It can be time spent listening to music, reading, writing in your journal, or just sitting quietly.

Using art or words, describe a way in which *you* like to recharge your batteries.

5 SPEAK WITH GOD

The Hebrew word for "prayer," *t'filah*, comes from the same root as the word meaning "to judge." Our tradition teaches that when we pray, we judge ourselves. Prayer helps us see that we are created *b'tzelem Elohim*—in God's image—and helps us think about ways to improve.

The next time you're in services or learning prayers in religious school, speak to God about ways in which you can become a better person—a mensch!

A Note of Middot
CONTENTMENT

Based on the middah: "happy with one's lot"

Think about it: According to Jewish tradition, each of us is unique and has a unique purpose in the world. That means we are here for a reason! But it's hard to see that if we compare ourselves with others. A sure way to *lose* self-respect is to worry about being smarter, cuter, or happier than other kids.

Remember it: Knowing that we are *b'tzelem Elohim* helps us feel content with what we have—and who we are. When we are content with what we have, we have the confidence to stand up and say, "I am created in God's image, and I am important." The sages asked, "Who is rich?" Their reply? "The one who is happy with one's lot."

Chapter 5
Treating Yourself as a Mensch

Health

Moderation

Bodies and Minds

Self-discipline

Bodies, Baths, and Bicycles

Squeaky Brakes

The bad news is that your best friend is going to be at camp for the whole summer. The good news is that you get to borrow his brand-new eighteen-speed. As you cruise around the neighborhood, you marvel at how smoothly it climbs hills, glides around corners, and locks into gear. This bike is *amazing*. So amazing, you decide, that there's no need to find room in the garage; it'll be just fine in the driveway. So what if it's raining?

The next day, the chain grinds like someone chewing marbles. The rain must have un-greased the chain, you think, pedaling fast to get home before it *really* starts pouring. You drop the bike in the driveway, dash inside, and flop down on the couch. Moments later, Mom's car pulls into the driveway, crushing the bike's frame, firing spokes into the garage door.

As you look out the window, watching the eighteen-speed's rear wheel glide down the street, you realize you can't blame *this* on the rain. You have no choice but to blame your little sister.

THE BIKE WAS AWESOME.

A bicycle requires attention, maintenance, and care. How much more so your body, which is created in God's image? In order to treat yourself as a mensch, you must be a mensch to your body. That's why this chapter comes complete with tips and wisdom from our tradition to help *you* climb hills, glide around corners, and lock into gear.

✚ DR. GOODMENSCH ✚

Dr. Susie Goodmensch, world-famous bicycle-and-body doctor, is in for a busy day. Luckily she's got a great assistant: you. On each patient's Rx pad, write the numbers of two treatments you think will help. Then add one of your own.

PATIENTS

I'M SICK. WHAT SHOULD I DO?

CARLA

I SHOULD PROBABLY GET UP AND DO SOMETHING. ANY IDEAS?

IRA

I DON'T LIKE GOING TO THE DOCTOR. WHAT CAN I DO TO STAY AWAY?

LISA

TREATMENTS

1. **Get a good night's sleep!**
2. **Keep germs away by washing your hands—and the rest of your body, too!**
3. **Eat nutritious food, including lots of fruits and vegetables.**
4. **Exercise your body with physical activities that you enjoy!**
5. **Exercise your mind with a good book and by giving your all at school.**

✚ R$_x$ _____

Name: **CARLA**
Treatments:
#_____   #_____

Also, don't forget to:

_____
_____

✚ R$_x$ _____

Name: **IRA**
Treatments:
#_____   #_____

Also, don't forget to:

_____
_____

✚ R$_x$ _____

Name: **LISA**
Treatments:
#_____   #_____

Also, don't forget to:

_____
_____

Hillel's Mitzvah

According to legend, the sage Hillel had finished teaching when a student approached him and asked, "Where are you going?"

"To the bathhouse," Hillel replied, "to perform a religious duty."

"What religious duty could you possibly fulfill *there?*" asked the student.

"Bathing, of course," replied Hillel.

"I don't understand," said the student. "How is bathing a religious duty?"

QUICK QUOTE

The body is the instrument of the soul.
—*Maimonides, great rabbi and philosopher*

CAN I BE A MENSCH IF I DON'T CLEAN BETWEEN MY TOES? THAT TICKLES.

Hillel explained: "Think of those who clean and scour the statues of the king. Their work is considered an important, even noble responsibility. How much greater, then, is the obligation to care for the human body, which is created in God's image?"

Hillel understood that treating our bodies with respect is not only good for us—it is a mitzvah.

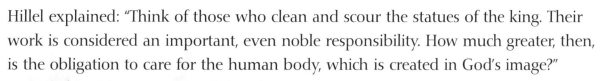

A Lifelong Loan
Think of your body as a loan from God. When we borrow something, we must take extra care to keep it in tip-top shape.

You can be a mensch to your body by eating healthy, nutritious food—like a warm, fresh pita stuffed with veggies.

To Your Health!

Be a Body Mensch

Sh'mirat habriyut—guarding one's health—is the "body mitzvah." Most of us practice *sh'mirat habriyut* every day, even though we may not know it: when we eat nutritious food, when we exercise, when we get a good night's sleep, when we look twice before crossing the street, even when we clean behind our ears. Every time we treat our bodies with respect, we practice *sh'mirat habriyut*.

Let's place *sh'mirat habriyut* under the Mensch-ifying Glass:
* ✳ The word *sh'mirat* comes from the Hebrew root meaning "guard," "protect," or "care for."
* ✳ *Ha* means "the." *Briyut* means "health" or "healthiness." (In Israel when someone sneezes, the appropriate response is *labriyut*, "to your health.")
* ✳ When we practice *sh'mirat habriyut*, we "guard" our "health."

שְׁמִירַת הַבְּרִיאוּת

Mensch-Wise

The Torah provides rules for treating our bodies with respect. One such rule forbids us to "make gashes in the flesh" (Leviticus 19:28). That verse has created an interesting debate in the Jewish community: Should body piercing (including pierced ears) be permitted, or should it be considered "gashes in the flesh"? What do *you* think?

_____

_____

_____

All in the Mind

Have you ever tossed and turned through the night before a big test? Have you ever felt really nervous as a test was about to begin? Have you ever eaten a gallon of rocky-road ice cream because you didn't do well? *Sh'mirat habriyut* is not just about caring for our bodies. It also encourages us to understand how we react to stress, anxiety, and disappointment. In other words, it is about knowing how our bodies and minds work *together*.

Life is full of sticky situations. But we can influence—sometimes even control—our responses. One way to prepare for these sticky situations is by asking questions about how to handle them. Another way is by challenging ourselves to respond with smart, healthy choices—even when we're nervous or unhappy or not as well prepared as we'd have liked. No two people are the same, so no two people's choices will be the same. It's up to you to make good choices about caring for yourself—including how much ice cream you can eat before you'll feel sick.

YOU KNOW BEST

✦ **when you're hungry**
✦ **where you're itchy**
✦ **just how cranky you'll feel in the morning if you stay up too late (and how everyone within ten miles should beware!)**

Sh'mirat habriyut **reminds you that no one knows you better than** *you.*

QUICK QUOTE **A clever mind seeks knowledge.**
—*Proverbs 15:14*

Body-ography

What works best for *your* body and mind? Fill in the blank lines and circle the red choices that best describe *you*. Be honest!

The Basics

I usually get about _____ hours of sleep, which is (circle one):

  a. not enough.   b. just enough.   c. more than enough.

I feel good about myself when I eat _____.
My favorite exercise is _____, which I do:

  a. all the time.   b. sometimes.   c. almost never.

What Works for Me, What Doesn't

I'm usually in a good mood when I _____. I
tend to get nervous, though, when I'm _____.
I'm lazy when it comes to _____, but when
I'm _____, I put all my energy into it.

Looking Ahead

From now on, I'd like to:

  a. exercise more.   b. read more.   c. practice more.

One thing I *must* do less of is _____.
One new thing I can do for my body every day is
_____, because _____
_____.

MENSCH
SPOTLIGHT

Name: Yael Arad

Scene: It is the 1992 Olympic Games in Barcelona, Spain. Although Israel has competed in the Olympics for forty years, no Israeli athlete has won a medal.

Action: Eager to overcome what she calls her country's "mental barrier," Yael Arad steps onto the judo mat to face Germany's Frauke Eickhoff, the former world champion. The winner of that match is assured at least a bronze medal. With a swooping move in which she flips her opponent onto the mat, Arad defeats Eickhoff. With a shout of joy, Arad jumps into the arms of the Israeli team officials. Yael Arad—and Israel—have their first Olympic medal.

What made Yael Arad a mensch: Yael took the value of *sh'mirat habriyut* to a new level. For nine years, she prepared for this moment with seven hours a day of intensive training, including weight lifting, long-distance running, and sparring with members of the men's team. In order to fulfill her dream, Yael knew that she must treat her body and her mind with absolute respect.

It's a fact: In many countries, an Olympic medal is just another victory. In Israel, Yael Arad's medal inspired dancing in the streets and displays of fireworks. "The whole country," said one Israeli, "is upside-down with joy."

SHMIRAT HABRIYUT
TOP 5

Don't leave home without these five ways to become a world-class health-mensch:

1 EAT MENSCH FOOD

Did you know that the Talmud forbids Jews to live in a city that does not contain a vegetable garden? That's how important Jewish tradition considers a healthy and nutritious diet.

An unhealthy food I will eat less often: _____

A healthy food I will eat more often: _____

2 GET MOVIN'

Have you ever stopped to think how amazing the human body is? Every organ, every bone, and every muscle has its own function, and they all work together in harmony. No wonder our morning prayers include the line "I will praise You, God, for I am awesomely and wondrously made" (Psalms 139:14).

What better way to respect your body than to exercise? Exercise is good for your heart, your muscles, your organs—plus it helps to keep your mind sharp. Draw a line from each activity to the expression you're likely to have while doing it.

playing soccer		**playing baseball or softball**
skating	☺	**playing basketball**
playing hockey	😐	**swimming**
doing gymnastics	😠	**dancing**
running or racing		**other:** _____

3 SLEEP TIGHT

Sleep allows us to replenish our energy and stay alert. Sleep is so precious that—according to Jewish law—depriving a neighbor of sleep is considered stealing! Give yourself time every night for a solid snooze.

Just to think about: How do you relax at bedtime? What do you like to do or think about just before you fall asleep?

4 BE A DANGER DODGER

There are lots of smart ways to protect ourselves and avoid unnecessary risks, including:

a. wearing a bicycle helmet

b. buckling your seatbelt when you ride in a car, even in the back seat

c. choosing not to ski the Super Mammoth Alpine Slope if you're a beginner. The Talmud tells us, "When injury is likely, don't rely on a miracle."

Describe a time in your life when *you* were glad you played it safe.

_____

_____

_____

5 BALANCE YOURSELF

Most of us have at one time or another eaten way too much, stayed up way too late on a school night, or spent way too much time watching TV. Judaism's answer: moderation. Strike a healthy balance between work and play, veggies and potato chips.

The following blessing comes from the Asher Yatzar, a prayer in which we thank God for the blessings of the body. Read it to yourself in Hebrew or English. It's a great way to remember the importance of respect for our body.

בָּרוּךְ אַתָּה יְיָ רוֹפֵא כָל־בָּשָׂר וּמַפְלִיא לַעֲשׂוֹת.

Praised are You, Adonai, who heals and sustains the body in wondrous ways.

A Note of Middot
SELF-DISCIPLINE

Based on the middah: "a moderation of worldly pleasure"

Think about it: If you had a whole cake to yourself, would you eat it? If you could sleep all day and all night, would you? If you could spend every minute zoning out by the TV, would you? Why or why not?

Remember it: There are two kinds of discipline: the kind that comes from outside yourself (parents, teachers, coaches) and the kind that comes from within. The first kind teaches good habits and reminds you to work hard. The second kind, self-discipline, puts *you* in charge. It helps you control your health, your thoughts, even your happiness. It helps you make good choices. "Just as a captain guides a ship in the best course," Rabbi Yoḥanan taught us, "guide yourself to do the right thing."

Part Three
Be a Mensch to Others

Chapter 6

Ready, Set, Mensch!

I'm ready to be a mensch to others. How do I start?

How did *talmud Torah*—Jewish learning—save the Jewish people?

How does learning lead to action?

Chapter 7

Be a Mensch to Your Family

Why is *sh'lom bayit*—peace in the home—among our most important values?

How are our parents and God partners in Creation?

Why should I be nice to my siblings?

Chapter 8

Be a Mensch to Your Friends and Classmates

Why does Judaism require us to be a good friend?

How can arguing with friends be a good thing?

How does *dibbuk ḥaverim*—attachment to friends—make me a better person?

Chapter 9

Be a Mensch to Everyone

How can an act of kindness change the world?

How does shaking a *gragger* during Purim make me a mensch?

How is *k'vod habriyot*—respect for all people—contagious?

Chapter 6
Ready, Set, Mensch!

Learning

Teaching

Torah

Humility

Live and Learn

First Things First

You can read and understand this sentence, though it's really just a mishmash of squiggly black lines. You've become so good at translating these squiggles into ideas and images, in fact, that you can read squiggles of all sh**ape**s and sizes. You can read squiggles upside down, backward, even with some squggls mssng. You can read because you learned the alphabet, then you learned how letters combine into syllables and words, and then you practiced and practiced and practiced some more. Now you don't even think about the squiggly lines—you just read.

It's the same when it comes to being a mensch to others. Just as we learn to read, we learn to become someone who has a positive impact on those around us. That's why Part Three of *A Kid's Mensch Handbook*—the part about being a mensch to others—begins with a chapter on *learning*. After all, without learning, we couldn't do much of anything, could we? We couldn't tie our shoes, play checkers, or say "shalom." Learning is the way each of us collects the tools necessary to become a mensch.

> MY FAVORITE SQUIGGLES LOOK LIKE THIS: CAKE

QUICK QUOTE **When I pray, I talk to God. When I study, God talks to me.**
—Rabbi Louis Finkelstein, American scholar

The Tree of Knowledge

Learning is like a seed. It starts out small—as an idea, a conversation with a friend, a line from Torah. Then it grows. It becomes knowledge, then plans, then action. Track the "learning seeds" in your life by completing the chart below.

Favorite Teacher	Skill He or She Taught Me	What I Can Do Now
Mr. Weiss	To read Hebrew	Blessing over candles

Relative or Friend	Lesson He or She Taught Me	What I Know Now
Grandma	Don't gossip.	Words can hurt.

Learning to the Rescue

Two thousand years ago, the Jewish people experienced a great tragedy: The Romans destroyed the Holy Temple in Jerusalem. Jews no longer had a "home base" at which to worship or gather for festivals. Jewish communities had no capital, no army, and no land to unite them. Judaism was faced with its most difficult challenge: How can we stay together if we do not share a home?

The Torah helps to keep the Jewish people strong.

The rabbis had an answer: learning. If everyone would learn the Torah and live by its teachings, it wouldn't matter where Jews live; everyone would be on the "same page." And so the Torah took the place of the Holy Temple as the authority on Judaism's beliefs, history, and law. Unlike the Holy Temple, the knowledge contained in the Torah could not be destroyed. Plus, the Torah was portable—it could be taken anywhere. As long as Jews learned from it, the Torah would be their "home base."

I CAN STUDY TORAH ANYWHERE, EVEN IN HAWAII. ALOHA!

QUICK QUOTE Learning, learning, learning: That is the secret of Jewish survival.
—Aḥad Ha'am, Russian Zionist leader

MENSCH SPOTLIGHT

Name: Akiva ben Joseph

Scene: It is about two thousand years ago, during the Roman Empire. Jews are forbidden to study Torah. Those who break the law are arrested. Sometimes they are even put to death. Rabbi Akiva is one of the greatest Jewish teachers and scholars of all time. His explanations and organization of Jewish law will be used for thousands of years.

Action: Rabbi Akiva ignores the decree forbidding Jews to study Torah. Asked why he would risk his life in this way, Rabbi Akiva explains, "Just as fish need water to live, so the Jewish people need the Torah. Though it may be dangerous to continue studying, it would be far more dangerous to stop." And Rabbi Akiva returns to his studies.

What made Rabbi Akiva a mensch: Rabbi Aviva understood the importance of learning to the Jewish people—and was willing to risk his life for it.

It's a fact: For most of his life, Rabbi Akiva was a shepherd. He could hardly read or write. It wasn't until he was forty years old that he began to study Torah.

Planting the Seed

The Most Important Mitzvah

For thousands of years, the mitzvah of Jewish learning, *talmud Torah*, has been an important part of Jewish life—more important than prayer, more important than fasting, more important than observing Shabbat. *Talmud Torah* has reminded us, from generation to generation, of the importance of living peaceful lives and of treating one another with compassion and respect. *Talmud Torah* is so important, in fact, that tradition considers it the single most important mitzvah.

Before we explore why, let's look at *talmud Torah* under the Mensch-ifying Glass:

* ✳ The word *talmud* comes from the Hebrew root meaning "study" or "learn."
* ✳ *Torah* usually refers to the Five Books of Moses (Genesis, Exodus, Leviticus, Numbers, Deuteronomy), but it can also refer to all Jewish learning, including the study of Hebrew, Jewish history, and the State of Israel.
* ✳ We usually translate *talmud Torah* as "Jewish learning."

תַּלְמוּד
תּוֹרָה

Once we learn, we can do.

The Great Debate

This famous debate between two great rabbis helps to explain the unique importance of *talmud Torah*: Rabbi Tarfon and Rabbi Akiva were studying Torah when the question was posed, "Which is greater, learning or action?" Rabbi Tarfon replied, "Action is greater." Rabbi Akiva disagreed. He said, "Learning is the more important of these two, because learning leads to action."

IF I LEARN TO MAKE PIZZA, I CAN EAT IT EVERY DAY.

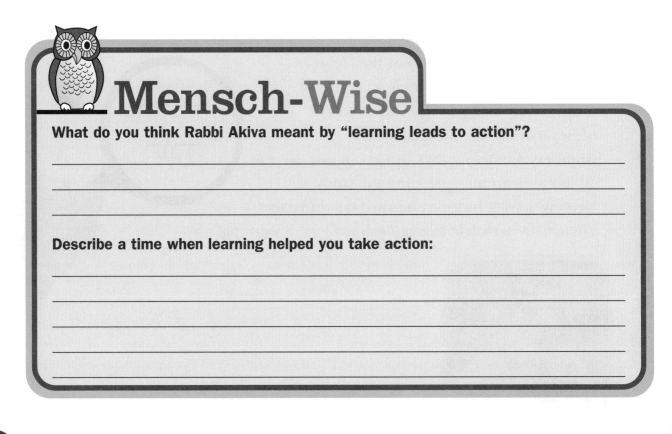

Mensch-Wise

What do you think Rabbi Akiva meant by "learning leads to action"?

_____

_____

_____

Describe a time when learning helped you take action:

_____

_____

_____

_____

Mount Mitzvah

Climb Mount Mitzvah by connecting each mitzvah at level 1 to its action at level 2 and then to its result at level 3.

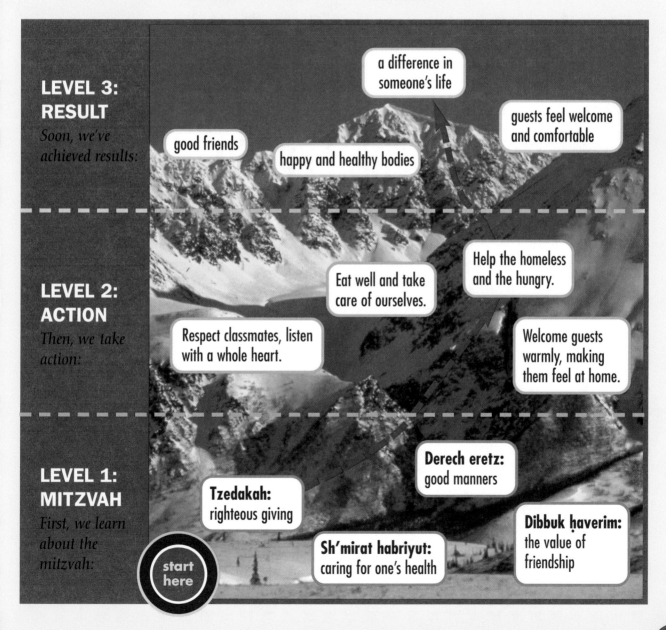

LEVEL 3: RESULT
Soon, we've achieved results:

a difference in someone's life

good friends

happy and healthy bodies

guests feel welcome and comfortable

LEVEL 2: ACTION
Then, we take action:

Eat well and take care of ourselves.

Help the homeless and the hungry.

Respect classmates, listen with a whole heart.

Welcome guests warmly, making them feel at home.

LEVEL 1: MITZVAH
First, we learn about the mitzvah:

start here

Tzedakah: righteous giving

Derech eretz: good manners

Sh'mirat habriyut: caring for one's health

Dibbuk ḥaverim: the value of friendship

TALMUD TORAH
TOP 5

Talmud Torah can be downright hard. It can also be energizing, amusing, and inspiring. These five tips are sure to help you make the most of your *talmud Torah* time:

1 FOLLOW THE LEADER

"Provide yourself a teacher," *Pirkei Avot* advises us. You know that the people who teach you math and Hebrew at school are teachers. But parents, siblings—even friends—can be teachers, too. Fill this box with words that describe a good teacher. We'll give you a head start:

patient   caring

2 STUDY WITH A BUDDY

Pirkei Avot also advises us to "acquire a friend" or "study companion." Describe *your* favorite study partner. How do you help each other learn?

_____

_____

_____

③ SET ASIDE TIME

Jewish tradition tells us that we should always set aside time for study. Because we often have so much to do after school, finding time can be hard. A schedule can help.

A. In the chart below, fill in your typical after-school schedule.

B. Place a ✔ next to the times when you do things that involve learning, such as homework or practicing a musical instrument.

C. Place a ✚ next to a time when you can fit in something extra, like reading a good book or brushing up on your Hebrew.

3 p.m. _____	5 p.m. _____	7 p.m. _____
4 p.m. _____	6 p.m. _____	8 p.m. _____

④ LEARN FOR FUN

Sometimes we learn because it's our job: We have to pass a test, earn a good grade, or remember our lines for the school play. Sometimes we learn simply because we *like* to. That's what Jewish tradition calls *Torah lishma*, "learning for the sake of learning."

Circle the subjects that *you* enjoy learning for the sake of learning. Draw an ✗ through subjects that you could . . . well . . . do without.

Math	Social Studies	Sports
Foreign Languages	English	Science
Music	Dance	Computers

5 PASS IT ON

Sometimes the best way to learn is by teaching. In order to pass knowledge on to others, you must be clear and accurate. There are many opportunities for *you* to teach. For example, you could help a sibling with spelling words, show a classmate how best to complete the math homework, or teach a younger Hebrew school student the *alef-bet*.

A *midrash* tells us, "As you teach, you learn." What do you think the rabbis meant by that?

Teaching can be fun for the students and the teacher.

_____

_____

_____

_____

A Note of Middot
HUMILITY

Based on the middah: "not boasting of one's learning"

Think about it: You can't believe that you just received a good grade on your science test. You want to write on the chalkboard, "I am gifted! I am a genius!" But from the looks on your classmates' faces, you guess that they didn't do as well. Will bragging about your grade help them? Will it help *you*?

Remember it: According to legend, the *yud* י made itself the smallest letter in the Hebrew alphabet in order to bring honor to the letters around it. As a reward, the *yud* became holy among the letters and a symbol of God's name יְיָ . Our tradition teaches us to be like the *yud*: to avoid arrogance and self-praise and to bring honor to others rather than to ourselves. *Saying* you have learned to help others doesn't make you a mensch. *Helping them* does.

Chapter 7

Be a Mensch to Your Family

Peace

Honor

Harmony

Patience

Family Matters

The Family Mensch

Imagine this: It is biblical times, and you are Joseph. You're strutting around in the gift your father just gave you: a coat of many colors. Your eleven brothers, who received nothing, are crazy with jealousy. The next day, you tell your family about a dream you had—of the sun, the moon, and eleven stars bowing down to you. Your family, especially your eleven brothers, do not like your dream. Soon after, your brothers throw you into a pit, sell you into slavery, and tell your father that you were eaten by a wild animal. They even have the blood-stained coat of many colors to prove it.

I HAVE SOCKS OF MANY COLORS.

Except for the dreams in which your siblings are bowing down to you, your family life is probably quite different from Joseph's. You know the importance of working together, of being patient, and of treating one another with respect. Most important, you know that you are an important person in your family—and that your family depends on you to

play fair   respect privacy   be tolerant.

do your part   be kind

In this chapter you'll learn how doing those things make you what may be the most important kind of mensch: a family mensch.

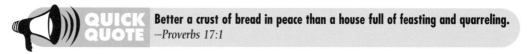

QUICK QUOTE Better a crust of bread in peace than a house full of feasting and quarreling.
—*Proverbs 17:1*

✿ Home Sweet Home ✿
What's *your* family like?

1 The Basics

Names of your family members:

If you have siblings, where do you fit in (were you firstborn, the second, the ninth)?

Do you consider the size of your family large, medium, or small?

2 Your Unique Family

Describe a way in which your family is special or unique.

What about your family makes you most proud?

3 Your Role

Circle the choice that best completes this sentence: When it comes to helping around the house, I am:

a. very helpful   c. not very helpful
b. kind of helpful   d. a total lump

In what ways are you like the other members of your family?

In what ways are you unique in your family?

4 Your Effect

Circle the choice that best completes this sentence: When it comes to my family, I am

a. respectful and   c. mean and stubborn
   loving   d. all of the above—
b. nice enough   it depends on the
                        day

Would your family agree with your answer? Why or why not?

Shalom at Home

The Magic Word

Shalom may have been the first Hebrew word you learned. You know that it can mean "hello" or "goodbye," depending on whether you're coming or going. You also know it can mean "peace." But did you know that *shalom* is related to the words for "completeness" and "harmony"? That's why the Jewish value of *sh'lom bayit*—peace in the home—means much more than "quiet house." It teaches us to seek *shalom* in the place where it's most important.

> SHALOM CAN ALSO MEAN "HOWDY."

What a Value!

Sh'lom bayit is such an important value, Rabbi Natan told us, that "if one brings peace into the home, it is as though peace were brought to all Israel."

Let's look at *sh'lom bayit* under the Mensch-ifying Glass:

* In this phrase, we usually translate sh'lom (shalom) as "peace."
* Bayit means "house" or "home." It can also mean "family."
* When we have *shalom* in our *bayit*, we have *sh'lom bayit*—a peaceful home.

שָׁלוֹם
בַּיִת

Mensch Cake Recipe

- From the list of ingredients, choose the three that you consider most important for creating *sh'lom bayit* in your home.
- Write the ingredients on the lines below.
- After each ingredient, explain why it is important for your mensch cake.

Ingredients

trust	respect for privacy	patience
sense of humor	respect for feelings	honesty
cooperation	other:_____	

Ingredient #1: _____

Reason: _____

_____

Ingredient #2: _____

Reason: _____

_____

Ingredient #3: _____

Reason: _____

_____

Mom and Dad: Partners in Creation

Four hundred years ago, Rabbi Loew of Prague made this observation of the Ten Commandments: Those on the first tablet, such as *Do not pray to idols* and *Do not use My name in vain*, are about our relationship with God, while those on the second tablet, such as *Do not steal* and *Do not murder*, are about our relationships with other people. The one exception is the fifth commandment, *kibbud av v'em*—Honor your father and mother— which appears on the first tablet. Rabbi Loew explained: "When we honor those who created us, we also honor the One who created the world itself." God and our parents, Rabbi Loew taught, were partners in our creation.

Sh'lom bayit begins with our parents. Not only because they feed us when we're hungry, cheer us up when we're sad, and do a thousand other things in between, but also because they link us to our sacred past, our culture, and our Covenant with God. It's impossible to achieve *sh'lom bayit*, our sages taught us, unless we're a mensch to Mom and Dad.

There is no gift parents appreciate more than **sh'lom bayit.**

Brothers and Sisters: Friends for Life

Getting along with siblings has always been tough. Just look in the Torah:

- ✦ **Cain hated Abel, then killed him.**
- ✦ **Esau was angry with Jacob and *threatened* to kill him.**
- ✦ **Rachel was so jealous of Leah that she considered killing *herself*.**
- ✦ **Joseph and his brothers? Well, we know about *them*.**

Moses and Aaron, however, had a different experience. They remained friends throughout their lives. When Moses needed help speaking to Pharaoh, Aaron was there. When God honored Aaron by making him High Priest, Moses was proud. Of Moses and Aaron the Psalms tell us, "How good and pleasant it is for brothers to live together in unity."

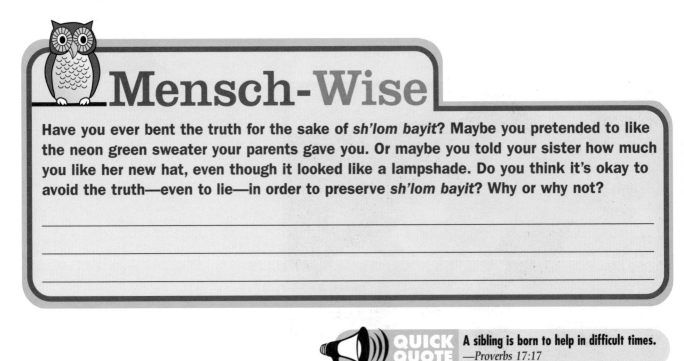

Mensch-Wise

Have you ever bent the truth for the sake of *sh'lom bayit*? Maybe you pretended to like the neon green sweater your parents gave you. Or maybe you told your sister how much you like her new hat, even though it looked like a lampshade. Do you think it's okay to avoid the truth—even to lie—in order to preserve *sh'lom bayit*? Why or why not?

_____

_____

_____

QUICK QUOTE A sibling is born to help in difficult times.
—*Proverbs 17:17*

KEEP OUT!

Jewish tradition tells us, "Do not enter your neighbor's premises without permission."

A key to *sh'lom bayit* among siblings is respect for one another's privacy.

You may know what it's like to fight with a brother or sister. You may also know that those clashes can challenge *sh'lom bayit*—for you *and* for your parents. But by sticking up for your little brother or respecting your big sister's privacy or putting up with your other brother's nonstop whining (at least sometimes), you can create a special connection that will bring your family joy—and strengthen *sh'lom bayit*—for a lifetime.

LET ME GET THIS STRAIGHT. MY SISTER IS ANNOYING BUT USEFUL.

SH'LOM BAYIT
TOP 5

Become your family's peacemaker in five easy steps:

1 ALWAYS SPEAK RESPECTFULLY TO MOM AND DAD.

As we grow up, we develop lots of opinions: how important our homework is, how neat our rooms need to be, how often we need to bathe. When our parents disagree, *sh'lom bayit* can be at risk. Jewish tradition teaches that it's important to honor our parents' requests—or at least protest in a kind and helpful way.

I SPEAK RESPECTFULLY TO MY PARENTS:

	Yes	No	Depends
when I want something	☐	☐	☐
when I'm happy	☐	☐	☐
when I'm angry	☐	☐	☐
when other people are around	☐	☐	☐

"When we honor our parents," our tradition teaches us, "we also give honor to God."

2 BE A TEAM PLAYER

Just like a sports team, your family relies on you to play your position well. Be it mowing the lawn, setting the table, or feeding the beagle, your family counts on you to field the ball when it comes your way.

Tell about a time when you did *not* fulfill a family responsibility and the *shalom* left your *bayit*. Then, describe a different way you could have handled the situation.

_____

_____

_____

3 DO FUN FAMILY STUFF

Whether it's playing games, sizzling latkes, or just talking about memories, time together can strengthen family peace.

Draw or write about a favorite Jewish family experience.

4 FORGIVE AND FORGET

Last week, your sister ate the last ice-cream sandwich when she *knew* it was yours. You would stop talking to her, except she had already stopped talking to *you* after you pulled her hair three weeks before. Apologizing and forgiving are hard. But being stubborn hurts *sh'lom bayit*. You don't have to wait until Yom Kippur to make up with people. Do it today.

Why is it sometimes hard to forgive? Write about a way to make forgiving easier.

_____

_____

_____

5 BE A FAMILY REP

Respect for yourself and respect for your family work together. When you recognize that you are created *b'tzelem Elohim*—in God's image—you respect yourself and others. As a result, people respect *you*.

Tell about a compliment you received recently (not about your hair or clothes, but about *you*). How was it also a compliment to your parents or to your family?

_____

_____

_____

_____

A Note of Middot
PATIENCE

Based on the middah: "slowness to anger"

Think about it: During the High Holidays, as we take the Torah from the Ark, we pray that in the coming year we may practice *erech apayim*—slowness to anger. We remember last year's temper tantrum, hurtful language, and grumblings about things so unimportant that now we can't even remember what they were.

Remember it: Think about ways to be more patient. Perhaps it means counting to ten before saying something hurtful, something you might want to take back. Perhaps it means simply saying, "Hey—It's no big deal." As the *midrash* tells us, "An angry person's words spill like boiling water from a kettle." A mensch does not allow anger to burn others. A mensch is patient.

Chapter 8

Be a Mensch to Your Friends and Classmates

Honesty

Compromise

Cooperation

Kindness

The Greatest Gift

Superfriend

In second grade, Rachel's classmates thought she was peculiar. She was friendly to *everyone*, even the "weird" kids. "How could you talk to them?" her friends would ask. "*He's* gross, and *she* wears funny sneakers." "I don't care," Rachel would answer. "But *she* can't play kickball." "I don't care." "And *he's* just so . . . *strange*." "I don't care," Rachel would say, because she really didn't.

In fifth grade, Rachel's classmates elected her class president—unanimously. Each student in the class had a different reason why, including:

- ✦ **Rachel talked to me when no one else would.**
- ✦ **Rachel keeps secrets.**
- ✦ **Rachel is interested in me, not just herself.**
- ✦ **When kids gossip about someone, Rachel sticks up for that person—or walks away.**

I CAN KEEP A SECRET, TOO. JUST NOT FOR VERY LONG.

Rachel was a great class president. She formed the New Kid Welcoming Committee, started an online homework-help message board, and with the support of the principal started music, art, and computer clubs so that kids could meet and share their interests. When the school year was over, her classmates presented her with a thank-you card. It was easy to write: "To Rachel, for showing us how to be a friend."

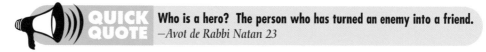
QUICK QUOTE Who is a hero? The person who has turned an enemy into a friend.
—Avot de Rabbi Natan 23

Mensch-o-meter

What qualities do you look for in a friend? Draw a line from each quality to its level of importance on the mensch-o-meter.

Level of Importance

VERY IMPORTANT
(I almost always look for these qualities in a friend.)

KIND OF IMPORTANT
(I sometimes look for these qualities in a friend. It depends.)

NOT THAT IMPORTANT
(I never look for these qualities in a friend.)

Quality

Honesty
(tells the truth)

Sense of Humor
(makes you laugh)

Common Interests
(likes the same stuff as you)

Popularity
(is liked by other people)

Trustworthiness
(keeps your secrets)

Kindness
(is nice to you and others)

Intelligence
(is a smart cookie)

Which of the above qualities do you think people like in *you*? Explain your answers.

1. _____

_____

2. _____

_____

3. _____

_____

Friend for Sale

There are few Jewish values as treasured as friendship. Friendship eases our burdens, allows us to see ourselves and the world in new, exciting ways, and makes ordinary things fun. Friendship makes life sweeter.

In fact, our sages taught us that friendship is not only important but *essential*. *Pirkei Avot* requires us to *k'nei*, "acquire" or "buy," a friend. *Buy a friend?* What's that? In the same way we might buy a CD or a hat or a pound of bananas? Or is it that we should buy a friend with gifts and excessive compliments, hoping to impress him or her? No. Instead, we

+ **spend time to build trust and loyalty.**
+ **give of ourselves by being open, honest, and generous.**
+ **pay attention—and listen with a whole heart.**

> I'LL TAKE TWO PACKS OF GUM AND FOURTEEN FRIENDS, PLEASE.

In order to *buy* a friend, *Pirkei Avot* teaches us, we must *be* a friend.

But that's not all *Pirkei Avot* has to say on the subject of friendship.

"Friendship," wrote Joseph Zabara, a Spanish poet, "is like one heart in two bodies."

Sticking Together

A Treasure

Pirkei Avot lists forty-eight values that are necessary to live a full life, a life of Torah. Included among them are study of Torah, love for humanity, and trust in the ancient sages. But *Pirkei Avot* also lists a more modest goal, one that each of us can achieve every day: *dibbuk ḥaverim*—attachment to friends.

Let's look at *dibbuk ḥaverim* under the Mensch-ifying Glass:

* *Dibbuk* comes from the Hebrew root meaning "cling," "attach," or "join." Another form of the word means "glue."
* *Ḥaverim* is the plural of *ḥaver*, meaning "friend." The word *ḥaverim* comes from the Hebrew root meaning "unite" or "blend."
* There are a number of ways to translate *dibbuk ḥaverim*: "clinging to friends," "joining with friends," even "sticking together."

דִּבּוּק
חֲבֵרִים

We fulfill the value of *dibbuk ḥaverim* when we respect our friends by listening to their opinions. Or when we appreciate them by fussing over their birthdays. Or when we honor them by keeping their secrets. Whenever we treat our friends as *we* wish to be treated, we honor the value of *dibbuk ḥaverim*—and take a giant leap toward mensch-hood.

 **QUICK QUOTE** A faithful friend is a powerful defense. The person who has found such a friend has found a treasure. —*Ben Sira 6:14*

Win-Win

In the Book of Samuel, the prophet Nathan criticizes his friend King David for causing the death of an innocent man. It must have been hard to confront his friend (and his king), but Nathan was bold: "Why have you ignored the command of God?" he asked David. The king could have become angry or given excuses for his actions or even had Nathan killed—anything to avoid admitting a mistake. Instead, David realized that what he had done was wrong, and he expressed gratitude for Nathan's friendship. "I stand guilty before God," David told his friend. In that way, Nathan helped David to become a better person.

Friendship is different from other relationships. Unlike our family and neighbors, we choose our friends, and we earn the privilege of having them in our lives. Because of its unique nature, the rewards of friendship—for you *and* for your friends—are uniquely precious. Friendship is a win-win situation.

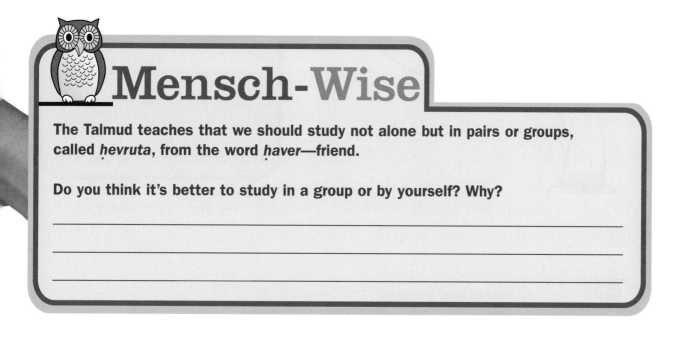

Mensch-Wise

The Talmud teaches that we should study not alone but in pairs or groups, called ḥevruta, from the word ḥaver—friend.

Do you think it's better to study in a group or by yourself? Why?

_____

_____

_____

Maybe you've had a friend who inspired you to think in a different way. Maybe he invited everyone to his birthday party, even the kids he didn't know. Maybe she was quiet while others bragged about their science test, even though you knew she got an A+. Maybe your friend challenged you—even corrected you (hopefully in a kind way)—to help you realize that you had been unfriendly or unfair. You may have felt hurt or uncomfortable at the time but grateful later, when you realized your friend had helped you make a better choice.

I WOULD HAVE GOTTEN AN A+ ON THE SCIENCE TEST, BUT I BLEW UP MY BEAKER.

A Friend Indeed

Tell about a time when a friend helped *you* to become a better person or a better friend. How did it feel?

_____

_____

_____

_____

_____

_____

_____

_____

_____

_____

_____

_____

Through friendship, we can help one another to improve—and reach our own greatest potential.

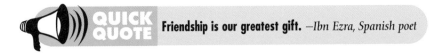 **QUICK QUOTE** **Friendship is our greatest gift.** *—Ibn Ezra, Spanish poet*

DIBBUK ḤAVERIM TOP 5

Here are five ways to create new friendships, strengthen old ones, and make *dibbuk ḥaverim* part of your regular routine:

1 BE FRIENDLY

Sounds simple, right? Not always. It takes courage to say the first hello. But you never know where that hello might lead! It might be the last word you ever say to someone, or it may be the first of a million words.

Benjamin Mandelstamm, a Jewish novelist, wrote, "Friendship is like a bank; you cannot take from it more than you put in." Describe an example from your own life that explains this point.

_____

_____

_____

_____

_____

_____

2 MEET IN THE MIDDLE

The Hebrew word for "compromise," *p'sharah*, comes from the same root as *pashor*, the word for "melt." When we compromise, it's as if we melt our wishes with our friend's, creating something new.

Compromise Quiz

You and a friend have sixty minutes before dinner. You want to watch an hour-long TV show. Your friend wants to play one-on-one basketball. You both have lots of homework to do after dinner. Propose three ways to spend the time:

1. _____

2. _____

3. _____

3 KEEP A SECRET SAFE

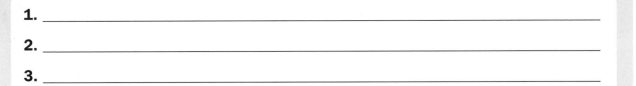

When it comes to friendships, trust is a must. We rely on one another to keep secrets and promises. That's why Judaism teaches us to avoid *l'shon hara*—gossip. When we gossip, we betray the trust of our friends, both those we gossip *about* and those we gossip *to*. That's why the writer Shlomo Rubin said, "Gossip is loved. The gossiper is hated."

Think of a secret you don't want anyone to know. (Don't write it down!) Imagine how it would feel if everyone around you knew your secret. That's how hurtful *l'shon hara*—gossip—can be.

4 LISTEN UP!

Kavanah means "concentration" and "focus." *Kavanah* helps us pass a test, practice an instrument, and hit a baseball. Friendship, too, requires *kavanah*. If while a friend is speaking, your mind wanders to a favorite video game or tomorrow's soccer match, *kavanah* is lost, and you haven't been a good friend. When a friend speaks, you should listen—*really listen.*

According to the Book of Ecclesiastes, "There is a time for silence and a time for speaking." In your own words, what does that verse mean?

_____

_____

_____

_____

_____

_____

_____

_____

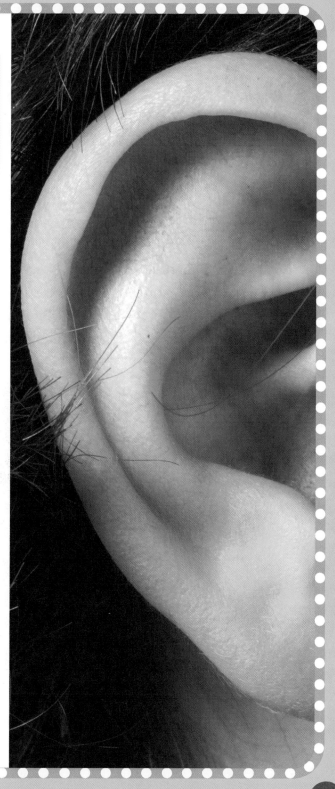

5 BE GRATEFUL FOR YOUR FRIENDS

Judaism provides a blessing to help us show our gratitude when we encounter a friend we haven't seen for a long time:

בָּרוּךְ אַתָּה יְיָ אֱלֹהֵינוּ מֶלֶךְ הָעוֹלָם
שֶׁהֶחֱיָנוּ וְקִיְּמָנוּ וְהִגִּיעָנוּ לַזְּמַן הַזֶּה.

Praised are You, Adonai our God, Ruler of the world, who has given us life and sustained us and enabled us to reach this time.

Look familiar? It's the Sheheḥeyanu, the prayer we recite at other special moments, such as the first night of Ḥanukkah or when a baby is born. Why is seeing a friend a good opportunity to recite the Sheheḥeyanu?

_____

_____

_____

_____

_____

A Note of Middot
COOPERATION

Based on the middah: "sharing responsibility with one's friend"

Think about it: Without cooperation, we can't win a soccer game, play Beethoven's Ninth, or move even a very small piano. A little cooperation can go a long way—in helping family, friends, neighbors, and ourselves.

Remember it: As Jews, we're especially aware of the importance of cooperation. The pioneers of Israel cooperated when they created *kibbutzim* (farming communities) and made the desert bloom. We cooperate when we pray together during services, bake ḥallah with Grandma, or help a friend understand a homework assignment. Almost anything we do can be easier and more meaningful when we work with someone else. A mensch offers help and *cooperates*.

Chapter 9
Be a Mensch to Everyone

Manners

Community

Tzedakah

Happiness

One Piece at a Time

Nearly five hundred years ago, Rabbi Isaac Luria told this version of the world's creation:

In order to make room for the world, God took a deep breath. When God breathed out, divine light—brighter than a billion suns—burst forth and flowed into special containers, called vessels. But the divine light was too powerful. The vessels weakened, cracked, and shattered. Sparks of light and shards of the broken vessels scattered everywhere in a mixed-up, jumbled mess. Instead of being perfect, the world became subject to war, hatred, and cruelty.

But there was hope. It would be the job of every person—each in his or her own way—to repair the broken vessels. Only when we complete this work will the world be whole. But how? Through mitzvot. Through helping others to help themselves, through giving tzedakah, through treating others with respect. Each time we perform even the smallest mitzvah, we collect a piece of one of the broken vessels—and help repair the world.

> I'M HAPPY TO HELP REPAIR THE WORLD—AS LONG AS I DON'T HAVE TO CLEAN MY ROOM.

In this chapter, we'll discuss ways to be a mensch to people outside your circle of family and friends—to everyone in the world. We'll also discuss ways in which you improve the world without even knowing it.

QUICK QUOTE The world needs every single human being.
—*Rabbi Baruch of Medziboz*

Repairing the World

Judaism has a name for the process of repairing the world: *tikkun olam*. Any time we help others or improve the world in some way, we perform *tikkun olam* and become God's partners in Creation.

In your own words, describe how a mitzvah can help to repair the world.

_____

_____

_____

Name three ways in which *you* can help to repair the world this week:

1. _____

2. _____

3. _____

Every Jewish person, tradition tells us, has been assigned a specific repair job—a way to improve the world—that no one else can do. What do you think *your* repair job might be?

_____

_____

_____

_____

_____

_____

_____

The Mensch Toolbox

Just as a carpenter requires a hammer, screwdriver, ruler, and glue, so a mensch requires tools for treating everyone with *kavod*—respect. Here are four tools no mensch should be without:

K'vod Habriyot: Respect for All People

Think of *k'vod habriyot*—respect for all people—as the *shamash*, the Hanukkah candle we use to light the others. Think of kindness, responsibility, generosity, community, compassion, love, justice, and peace as the other eight candles. Once we have *k'vod habriyot*, the flame of respect, we can light our eight candles—and a thousand candles more.

Let's look at *k'vod habriyot* under the Mensch-ifying Glass:

* *K'vod* is a short form of *kavod*—respect.
* *Habriyot* comes from the Hebrew root meaning "create." Sometimes it refers to all of God's creations, sometimes to human beings, who, the Torah tells us, are special among God's creations.
* We translate *k'vod habriyot* as "respect for all people."

כְּבוֹד
הַבְּרִיּוֹת

The Kavod Railroad

Respect is contagious. If you treat others with *kavod*, they will often jump aboard and do the same. In the chart below, follow the Kavod Railroad around the world.

✦ **December 19:** You write a thank-you note to your piano teacher, Mrs. Schwartz, who places it on her fridge. Mr. Schwartz sees the card, which has a picture of a tree on it, and remembers to buy a gift for his Uncle Mike's birthday: a tree in Israel!

✦ **March 13:** Mr. Gold watches as his assistant, Avi, plants Uncle Mike's tree and says, "Great work!" Avi, in a great mood, drops an extra shekel in the tzedakah box at school the next day.

✦ **May 28:** Avi's class votes to send their tzedakah money to Humane Society International, which helps protect animals around the world. The HSI will use the money to raise ten kittens that were born in an animal shelter *in your town*.

✦ **December 19:** It's the best Ḥanukkah present you've ever received: your own kitten. You name her Beethoven, after your favorite composer.

In your own words, explain how *kavod* can be contagious.

_____

_____

_____

_____

List three words that describe how you feel when someone treats *you* with kavod—respect.

1. _____   2. _____   3. _____

Derech Eretz: The Mensch Way

Human beings have a lot in common with other creatures: We eat, sleep, find food, then eat some more. But there are key differences. A flounder doesn't say "please." A squirrel doesn't invite friends to share its acorn collection. And a mongoose doesn't hold the door for other mongooses. Human beings are capable of respectful behavior—showing courtesy, being polite, using good manners—that sets us apart from our furry and slimy friends. Jewish tradition calls this everyday respect *derech eretz.*

Derech eretz takes many forms: Saying "thanks" or "you're welcome" or "good morning" (especially if no one else does) is *derech eretz.* Wearing nice clothes to services (instead of your T-shirt that says "Let's Go, Marlins") is *derech eretz.* Even leaving the last slice of pizza for the host of the party— who's been too busy to eat— is *derech eretz.*

Dogs may be smart, but only human beings practice derech eretz.

 **There is no better measure of intelligence than good behavior.**
—*Solomon Ibn Gabirol, Spanish poet*

Mensch Manners

The Talmud mentions these ways of practicing *derech eretz*:

- ✦ Wait until your guests have their food before taking any yourself.
- ✦ If you criticize, do so in a kind way—and in private.
- ✦ Knock before entering a home.
- ✦ Be the person who says hello first.

Think of a way in which you can practice *derech eretz* . . .

at home:

_____

_____

_____

at school:

_____

_____

_____

while visiting another country:

_____

_____

_____

Klal Yisrael: One Big Family

Each of us belongs to many communities. You may be members of your family, your school, your orchestra, and your sports team. You are citizens of your town and your country. As Jews, we belong to another community, a special one: *klal Yisrael*—the world Jewish community. Like any community, *klal Yisrael* relies on the actions of its members to remain strong.

Jews around the world have always felt a strong bond to one another. We pray together, study together, and celebrate together. We connect to one another through support for the State of Israel, the Jewish homeland. And though we may live in different countries, speak different languages, and celebrate Jewish holidays with different customs, we are all connected to one another because we are Jews. Being part of *klal Yisrael* is like being a member of one big family.

There are many ways in which you can support the world Jewish community, both locally and globally:

QUICK QUOTE All Jews are responsible for one another.
—*Talmud, Shavuot 39*

✦ **Participate in programs at your synagogue, religious school, or camp.** Even by shaking a *gragger* at Purim services, you can help keep the Jewish community connected and strong.

✦ **Contribute to Jewish organizations.** Make tzedakah contributions to Jewish organizations, such as the Jewish Braille Institute, which helps blind people and people with impaired sight learn to read.

✦ **Go to Israel.** When the time comes, take a teen trip to Israel. There's no better way to show your support for the Jewish homeland.

These teenage Israeli scouts are proud representatives of klal Yisrael—*the world Jewish community.*

MENSCH SPOTLIGHT

Name: Henrietta Szold

Scene: It is the United States and *Eretz Yisrael*, between 1860 and 1945.

Action: Henrietta Szold becomes the first woman to be admitted to the Jewish Theological Seminary of America. She becomes a respected writer, editor, and educator. At age sixty, she moves to *Eretz Yisrael* in order to improve the conditions for thousands of Jewish pioneers. She insists on sharing modern medical knowledge and equipment with the Arabs of Palestine, even though the Jews and Arabs are political enemies.

Henrietta Szold also establishes, and serves as president of, Hadassah, an organization that is involved in the creation of the State of Israel (and is the largest Jewish organization in the world today).

What made Henrietta Szold a mensch: Szold contributed her talent and energy to *klal Yisrael*, the world Jewish community.

It's a fact: In honor of Henrietta Szold, Israel's Mother's Day is celebrated on her birthday.

Tzedakah: The Right Thing

Tzedakah is not charity. Charity is an important—but voluntary—act. If we feel generous, we can give charity. If we are saddened or moved by a needy cause, we can give charity. But as Jews, we are *obliged* to contribute time, talent, money—whatever we can—to those in need. We give tzedakah (from the Hebrew word meaning "righteous") because we have received much, because we have much to give, and because doing so is the right thing to do. No matter how we feel when we wake up in the morning, we give tzedakah.

Here are three ways to make tzedakah a part of your routine:

- ✦ **Place a tzedakah box in your home, perhaps on the kitchen counter. Declare that all loose change goes into the box. Then, every Rosh Hashanah, take a family vote to decide on that year's tzedakah recipient.**
- ✦ **Take part in a tzedakah project. Maybe your synagogue sponsors a park cleanup day or hosts a mitzvah day or serves Shabbat dinner at a local nursing home. With a rake or books or your family's famous matzah balls, you can change the world.**
- ✦ **Help the hungry and homeless with a special kind of tzedakah called *ma'achil r'evim*. You can fight hunger and homelessness on a local level by donating food to a homeless shelter, or on a global level by contributing to organizations such as the World Food Program, which distributes food to hungry people around the world.**

QUICK QUOTE *I always give much away, and so gather happiness instead of pleasure.*
—*Rahel Levin Varnhagen, German writer*

TZEDAKAH SUPREME

Maimonides defined these eight levels of tzedakah:

LEAST PRAISEWORTHY

1. Giving unwillingly
2. Giving cheerfully, but less than you should
3. Giving after being asked
4. Giving before being asked
5. Giving when you do not know the recipient, but the recipient knows you
6. Giving when you know the recipient, but the recipient does not know you
7. Giving when you do not know the recipient, and the recipient does not know you
8. The best kind of tzedakah, Maimonides taught, is when you help others to help themselves. Teach your brother or sister a new skill. Help someone find a job. Extend a gift or a loan for education or for a new business. In that way, you help others develop tools and self-respect, gifts that will last a lifetime.

MOST PRAISEWORTHY

Mensch-Wise

Which is more praiseworthy: donating a lot of money to a homeless shelter in order to appear generous or donating a small amount of money in order to feed the shelter's residents? Explain your answer.

_____

_____

_____

Mensch Magic

Like a stone on a still lake, your actions create ripples that roll outward: to your family, to your friends, to the whole world. Then, after a moment, the lake becomes still again. The ripples are gone.

Or are they?

One of the challenges of being a mensch lies in the fact that we often don't see the effect we've had on the world. We don't see *what happens next*. We may teach someone the *alef-bet* but not see the pride in her parents' eyes when she reads from the Torah for the first time. We may say thank-you to our school principal but not see the sunny mood that he and his family enjoy for the rest of the day.

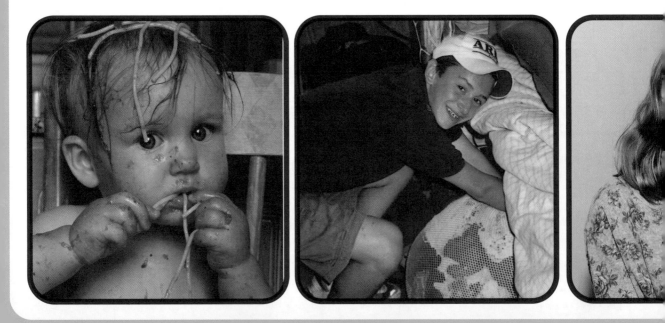

We may participate in a tzedakah fund-raiser but not see the smiling faces of those we've helped to feed.

Yes, sometimes we receive clues that we've hit the mark: a warm smile, a thank-you, a new friend. People may compliment us, look up to us, or—better yet—follow our example. But being a mensch isn't about receiving acknowledgment. It's about being a mensch *just because*. And *that's* where mensch magic comes in:

- ✦ **Mensch magic** is the magic of knowing that we can affect the world in unique and extraordinary ways.
- ✦ **Mensch magic** is the magic of making a difference in people's lives.
- ✦ **Mensch magic** is the magic of belonging to a rich and ancient heritage, one that recognizes that each of us is valuable beyond measure—and that our lives *matter*.
- ✦ **Mensch magic** is the magic of a special kind of happiness, deep in our soul.

Now, take what you've learned and make your own, mensch-ful *splash*!

MENSCH

Earn your mensch diploma by writing each Jewish value in the correct space.

respect for all people	attachment to friends	peace in the home
the Jewish community	righteous giving	in God's image
choices	"mensch manners"	good person
		respect

Freshman Mensch

I have learned that a mensch is a person of integrity, honor, and respect. In other words, a mensch is a

_____. I understand that a mensch makes good

_____ and then follows them up with action.

Sophomore Mensch

I recognize that each of us is created *b'tzelem Elohim*—

_____.

Because I am unique and contain a spark of the divine,

I have self-_____.

DIPLOMA

Junior Mensch

I practice *sh'lom bayit*—_____,
and *dibbuk ḥaverim*—_____.
I learn how to treat others with *kavod*.

Senior Mensch

I combine everything I've learned with a dose of
derech eretz—_____; tzedakah—
_____; and support for *klal Yisrael*—
_____. My self-respect has grown
into *k'vod habriyot*—_____.

On this day of _____, let it be known
date
that _____ has become
name
a mensch graduate—*mazal tov*!

Handy-Dandy Mensch Index

Respect for all people (*k'vod habriyot*)

Respect for one's health (*sh'mirat habriyut*)

Self-Discipline

Self-Respect

Tzedakah